T0114849

DARLA JUNE:
"TAILS FROM THE FAMILY DOG"

ROBIN STERLING

author HOUSE

AuthorHouse™
1663 Liberty Drive
Bloomington, IN 47403
www.authorhouse.com
Phone: 833-262-8899

Published by AuthorHouse 02/28/2021

ISBN: 978-1-6655-1849-9 (sc)
ISBN: 978-1-6655-1851-2 (e)

Print information available on the last page.

Any people depicted in stock imagery provided by Getty Images are models, and such images are being used for illustrative purposes only. Certain stock imagery © Getty Images.

This book is printed on acid-free paper.

I've wanted to tell my story since I was young, or in human terms, a puppy, pup, pumpkin, munchkin, bubbas, baby (that one really seems to have stuck the best), or any other silly, made-up version of my name my humans use in just about any situation. Whatever name they call me it wouldn't matter. I did then and still do answer to all of them. Every time.

This is probably a good spot to answer a few of the questions I will NOT be discussing because, well, they are just silly:

1. Who's the good girl? Answer: I am
2. Who's the baby? Answer: Again, I am
3. Who's the best baby in the whole wide world? Answer: Should be obvious by now but ok, I'll play along - I am.
4. Who's hungry? Answer: Me. Always.
5. Do I want any of the following: chewy, cookie, treat, peanut/peanut butter, anything remotely resembling YOUR food? Answer: YES, always - stop asking, just gimme.
6. Did I "do that"? Answer: If you are referring to something you know YOU didn't do - then DUH on you.
7. Where's the ball? Answer: Where I left. You go get it.
8. Was that you??? Answer: Yes, I tooted. Deal with it.

One more thing that should be mentioned because it really isn't silly at all. When my humans look at me and make sure I'm looking back at them and they tell me how much they love me; I know they mean it. They know me so well that when I do my "slow blink" (signature move) back to them, they hear my words. They know how madly in love I am with them, all of them. My humans love me more than any other animal or human in the world. I was one of the lucky ones, but it didn't start out that way.

RIGHT OFF THE TRUCK

Where my memories start, besides what I just ate, is a bit of a blur. I have heard my human, who I know as "Momma", say words to her humans that I was "tossed off the back of a truck" with my litter mates (whatever those are). We were left at a place where kids like us would be taken care of. That is not quite how I remember it.

I have one sister and four brothers. I was always closest to my sister because boys can be kind of silly sometimes. At least that was true of most of my brothers. They would do the same things over and over again and keep getting into trouble. Actually, come to think of it, I think one of my brothers got us into our mess in the first place.

From the beginning, he refused to stop talking (or as humans say 'barking'). Day, night, whatever, it didn't matter he just never stopped. I remember hearing a small human yelling at a bigger, louder and meaner human, "Tell him to stop! He is driving me crazy!" Next thing I knew we were all tossed outside and left there with no food or water for what seemed like a really, really long time.

I was always hungry. Always thirsty. I ate grass A LOT because

it was the only thing that would fill up my belly. In later years, I heard my Momma say that I was eating grass because I wasn't feeling well. I wish I could have saved her that worry. I was eating it because I didn't trust, in the beginning, that I would get much of anything else to eat that day, or ever.

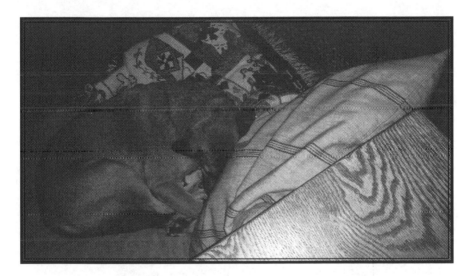

There were more tough days back then. Filled with various faces, none too friendly, that I saw only once, which was plenty. Then came the last of the lousy days. I remember being loaded into the back of something that moved fast and had lots and lots of twists, turns, and bumps. Looking back now I know this to have been my first car or on this day, truck ride. I didn't like it that day, but boy do I LOVE them now! More on that later.

All my brothers and my sister were with me. We huddled close to stay warm and to steady our little legs. We were all shaking not knowing what was coming next. After what seemed like eternity, the movement stopped but the truck still roared, it was still running.

Before I knew what was happening a huge, rough hand picked me up and put me into a dark, cold box on the ground. My sister came in next, landing directly on head. One after the other my brothers were lowered in until we were all in this box. Then the sounds were gone. We were all scared and shaking, it was the pits! Thankfully, this would not be our end but the first of much happier days!

SEEING THE LIGHT

I think we all fell asleep from pure exhaustion and trauma. When I started to wake up, I realized immediately that I was not in a dark box but a room filled with light. I looked around and only saw my sister, who was just waking up herself. She looked at me with fear in her eyes and I rushed to her side, that always made her feel better. I wondered where my brothers were. I hoped they were ok.

We had not been awake long before we both caught a whiff of something we very much wanted to find. It was the unmistakable smell of food. One slow step at a time, we began to search. As frightened as we were, let's be honest, we are dogs, food has always been a great motivator!

First, we came to a bowl filled with what looked like water, but we couldn't be sure. I dipped my little hoof in and took a sniff - it passed the test. I dove in and began to gobble up as much as I could as fast as I could. My sister eagerly joined me.

Once we had our fill of the water, we resumed our search for the food. We moved along together and locked in on the bowl at the same time. My sister was a bit more timid than me, so I tried it first. It would do just fine. I dropped a piece for her so she could see for herself.

Satisfied, we began to munch away and must have forgotten that we had no idea where we were. A squeaking noise came from the other side of the room and we both looked up in shock. I nudged my sister and we quickly backed into the first corner we could find. We began to shake again. More new humans, what if they were even worse than the last ones?

MY FIRST HUMANS

Through the open door, a male and a female were staring down at us with looks on their faces I had never seen. They almost looked sad but then they spoke to us very softly and said, "It's ok, we won't hurt you. No one will ever hurt you again, we promise."

Now, obviously I'm guessing about the exact words. I was so little then and knew almost no human words but when they spoke it was kind and I always imagined it was something like that. At any rate, they didn't frighten me. They even came in and sat on the floor so that we didn't have to look way, way up at them. That's something I've always loved. Sit with me and I'll kiss you for days. Some things never change.

The female reached her hand out toward me. I looked at my sister, who I knew would not move a muscle until I did, so I started to move slowly. I sniffed her hand, I remember it smelled like peanut butter, it was wonderful! As it turns out, peanut butter became my most favorite thing of all time! I kept going forward and before I knew it, she had started to pat my head so gently and she was smiling. I looked back to my sister and she knew it would be ok. She moved towards the male, who was just as gentle and kind. This day was getting better and better.

We all played together with toys and balls and they let us eat and drink as much as we wanted. Before we had settled in for the night, the male and female had begun to direct words to us that we had never heard before. When they used them, a different one for me than my sister, I could tell they wanted me to come towards them. It had been such a fun time and it was easy enough to do, so why not?

We were so tired, and the humans could tell. They showed us a pile of blankets and pushed our little bodies towards them. My sister and I climbed all around until we found the perfect spots. We cuddled together and looked up with grateful, yet tired eyes.

They looked down at us and said, "Goodnight Dory, goodnight Darla. We're so happy you're here!" I believed them. I also knew in that moment that I had a sister named Dory and I was Darla. Fine by me. Then we fell into a deep and wonderful sleep! The first of many, as it turned out.

FOLKS IN COATS

Not having any concept of time, I can't be clear on how long we were there with these humans. All I knew was that they cared for Dory and me like we were the best things since peanut butter, which is saying A LOT.

Not every day was dreamy, of course. But even on yucky bath days, they weren't so bad because I knew there would be a treat when it was over! When we went for a ride, this one much better and pleasant than my first one, we were excited. Then we met the folks in the coats that came with needles. Didn't love them, but they were still gentle enough and again a treat was provided afterwards, so, win/win. This is also when I discovered that becoming very still through these events helped me get through them quicker. This is a method I still use today.

Occasionally, I would wonder where my brothers had gone but figured they had been taken to a place much like this and were having a great time too. Even if it wasn't true, it helped me to think it was.

Dory had taken quite a shine to the male human. I was glad. He was fun and silly with her and she needed that. I bounced

around between them both because I just couldn't pick a favorite. I hoped my puppy days would be like this forever, whatever that was. Seemed like as soon as I had that thought, things changed. Boy, did they change.

MEETING MOMMA AND DADDY

One sunny cold morning, after I'd eaten, played and napped, something had changed. My humans were bringing things out to the car. Back and forth, in and out, each time the door opened the wind was colder than the last. Then I saw their faces. Just like the first time I saw them, they looked sad but in a different way.

The female came and scooped me up, hugging me closer to her than normal, and walked me out to the car. The male was already behind the circle thing that made the car twist and turn. I was placed in the back, like I had been before when we went to see the folks in coats.

I remember thinking, "Bummer, I guess it was time for another visit. At least there would be a treat in my future!" The thought had perked me right up!

As we drove, I was resigned to where this trip was taking me, then I looked out the window. I didn't recognize anything. I looked at my humans and realized they had been talking to me but I hadn't been listening, not until now.

The female had something glistening on her cheek that she kept wiping away. She was talking to me, she said, "You are going to love these guys. They are so excited to be getting you. We've told them how lucky they are and I believe they will just love you to pieces."

What was she talking about? Why wasn't Dory with us? It hadn't even occurred to me that she wasn't with us. Lucky Dory. She had the male wrapped around her little tail. Had I done something wrong? Was I too hyper? Did I talk too much? I kissed them too much. I knew it. That had to be annoying. It wasn't my fault, they always tasted salty and yummy. My thoughts were all over the place. Partly because I was so young but mostly because I was a dog and couldn't comprehend much more beyond pee, poop and treats.

The car came to a stop and I was staring at two new humans. They were smiling a lot. Like a real lot. Like the kind of smile I have when my belly gets rubbed or peanut butter has been dropped in my food dish. Huge smiles. My female opened the back door and called me over. Then the other smiling female picked me up and hugged me like I had never been hugged before. She twirled me around and began kissing my face and saying, "Oh Darla, I love you already!" Wow. She had the same wet stuff on her face that my female had. The new male petted my head and said, "Good looking pup, good girl." He was right, of course, but how did he know already? These were clearly exceptional humans. I remember wondering if I was being shared. Again, I was very young.

My humans surrounded this new female and whispered to me, "Now you be the best little girl Darla, ok? These two are your Mum and Daddy. They are going to take such great care of you. We will miss you but promise that Dory will be ok with us. Be good."

With that, they both kissed my head, one last pat. Now they

25

both had the wet stuff on their faces. I kissed them both, as I always had. Then I looked at my Mum and kissed her too. The wet stuff tasted salty, I liked it. I wondered if I was getting a treat for this. Yes, you can say it. Back then I wasn't the brightest bulb in the bunch, but I meant well.

In one sweeping moment, my humans were driving away, and I was sitting on my Mum's lap and my Daddy was holding onto the circle thingy with one hand and his other was patting my head. I knew very little at this point in my young life but what I never doubted from that day on was how very much my new humans, Mum and Daddy loved me. More than even peanut butter.

LUCKIEST DOG EVER

We had stopped moving. Mum was talking to me, saying a lot of the same things over and over, "You are the cutest, bestest baby ever!" You know, the usual. She was carrying me until Daddy spoke. He must have told her to put me down because right after he spoke, my hoofies hit the ground. I should mention that in my family, my hoofies are what I have heard other humans call "paws". How boring. My humans are never boring!

Anyway, I was off! I heard my Daddy say, "Go get your Momma! Where's Momma?" So, in that moment I knew two new things. First, my new female human was called "Momma" not "Mum". Second, I would follow her wherever she went. She had jogged ahead of me and I ran my hardest (little legs back then) to catch up. Then I saw it.

Oh my goodness, I had never seen anything like it. So. Much. Grass. I remember thinking that when the weather gets warmer I'll be on this all day, everyday. I wasn't wrong.

We all played together until it was time to go inside. I thought the outside was good, I had no way of knowing just how awesome my Momma and Daddy were. They walked me from room to room. They showed me so many things I could sleep on. Everything was soft! Everything was mine!

Then I felt something very, very warm on my behind. I turned around to see a thing I had never seen before. Instinctually I knew I needed to stay away from touching it. Too hot for my hoofies.

I watched as my Daddy put huge pieces of what I knew was wood into this thing, it was fascinating. Then I felt myself sit. Before I knew it, I was laying down. After that, I got nothing, fell asleep in record time. I was happy, tired and content. Then I heard the word I would come to know, oh so well, SUPPER. I was up like a shot. I have said it before, food is the best motivator! That was pretty much the only thing that would tear me away from my slumber in front of the hot thing. Still my favorite spot to nap.

WE ARE FAMILY

That first day will always be a favorite memory for me. As time has gone by, my parents (I learned that and lots of other words. My Momma says I'm wicked smart) have shown me a bunch of new things. Some I loved, like off leash hikes and walks! Some I didn't like so much, like water, totally not a fan. But every day has been different and fun and full of love. Sometimes I wonder if Dory and my brothers are doing ok, I tell myself they are. It helps me to think that, even now.

So, here I am, seven years old and wondering what else is in store for us. How can life get any better? Don't get me wrong there are days that aren't so fun. I've come to understand that Daddy goes away somewhere every now and then but Momma never gets mad. I am pretty sure it's legit. He's not leaving us behind, because he always comes home. Momma says the same thing to me if she's ever away, to help settle my mind. She says, "You hear this now Darla June Sterling (she uses my full name to make sure I'm listening), I will always come back for you. No matter what. Even if I go away for a little while I will always come back and so will Daddy, always." She has said it so many times that I think I believe her now.

I'd like to tell you how I got my full name. Well, you know where my first name came from and I'm pretty sure my last name

is the same as my parents. Not even sure how I know that but again, I'm wicked smart. My middle name, June, I share with my other favorite human, my Nana.

Want to talk love? I can't even go there without mentioning the spoils my Nana has shown me. From patient walks when I'm not "feeling my spot" to do my business, to special morsels of magic meat on every meal she prepares for me, my Nana loves me. And as a bonus she totally gets my obsession with peanut butter. Got my own spoon and everything.

Yup, Nana is awesome, love her like crazy. I keep a sharp eye out and protect her daily from horrible mail trucks and scary delivery people. She always tells me how beautiful and brave I am. I believe her. Nana doesn't lie.

My Momma wants to say a few words. I'm sure it'll be more of the usual. But stay, be good and maybe you'll get a treat afterwards too.

FROM MY MOMMA

As you can see, my baby girl (no matter how old she gets, she'll always be my baby) is quite special. The joy she has brought to our lives is immeasurable and our love is beyond the reach of galaxies. I could go on and on but I'm confident that Darla June has said it all.

I never knew much about her early days. She had buried those memories deep. The rescue where we found her filled in most of the blanks, but the details belong to Darla. She's a special pup. She has a way of making everyone feel loved.

For me, as her de facto Momma, I couldn't feel luckier. She's a blessing that we will cherish every single day of her life. She will always know love and I'll protect her with my life, as will her Daddy. We are family and that's what you do for family. We love you Darla June Sterling, more than you will ever know!

I got a treat - I got her.

Printed in the United States
By Bookmasters